Alfaaz

Zenia Elavia

Presentation by *BookLeaf Publishing*

Web: www.bookleafpub.com

E-mail: info@bookleafpub.com

ISBN: 9789358369588

First edition 2023

The True Winners

Set your goals, for as high as you want,
For the sky is the limit...

There are many lives yet to unfold, With stories
of success not yet told.
Stories of people born limbless,
But that doesn't make them aimless.
They live with greater vigor and passion, And
guide others in all manner and fashion

Stories of losers, who do not last,
Winners who learn from the past, Achievers who
work in the present,
To gain sure success in the future.

So go on, Find your dreams, Work incessantly
for it, Until you become a true achiever.
"For even the sky is no limit, For a winner's
endless endeavor"

Nostalgia

As I sat by the sea shore,
Glancing at the horizon,
The sun had just risen
The sound of waves lashing against the coast,
The cool breeze,
Touching my cheek
I turned to see,
I was already walking down the memory lane

Those good old school days
Certainly the best of life's maze
Innocent juvenile us
With never too much to fuss!

Kindergarten:The beginning of times
Some visuals can never be forgotten
Mother holding my hand,
And me closing my eyes and letting her carve my first ABC..
Her countless screeches, when I would eat sand

My hair pulled up into 2 ponytails
I was certainly mom's tail
KG wouldn't have had all the fantasm,

Without that boy, who put up with all my childhood tantrums

Primary School: No ray of hope
2 years of togetherness, had all gone in vain
The separation pain
Had just seeped in
When life threw me a curveball
I was no longer mom's adorable doll
Life revolved around Dictation
The childhood screeches now transformed into frustrated anger
"Spank her"
And the wrong spelling 'creepers'
Was forever etched to my mind

Middle School: The misery couldn't get any better
I finally had an edge over English
But failed to distinguish
Whether math was more alien or geography
The concept of girl friends
I certainly had a lot to comprehend
And way too many errands
Everyday struggle to catch the morning bus
The long school route
Is what my deprived sleep would any-day hoot
The overly disciplined
The well dressed

Every teachers' blessed
Ahh! Can't picturize myself any better ●

Senior School: All's well that ends well
My roller coaster life already met with an identity crises
I was the so called Boss girl's sister
I couldn't please any mister ●
But mom's early morning almonds, had certainly made me wiser
For Success came more naturally
And I fell in love yet again with Psychiatry

So close, yet so far!

Meet me in a poem,
Somewhere between the lines
Where the rhythm roams,
Find me in a verse,
Be sure to not get lost in the rhymes…
Look for me where emotion evoked phrases exist
Locate me where expression and imagination persist
O wait!
U can encounter me in your hcart,
And feel me in the art of my poems!

Hanging on

It's not often that one finds
In this messy world of blind
Dates and tinder one night stands;
A chance to look at true romance

And yet, what twisted random ploy;
While window shopping at Macy's in Chicago;
One comes across a sight-
Two lovers poised as only lovers might.
His arm wound tight around her waist
Her satin gown clings with delicate taste
Her body wrapped in his embrace
That hooked expression on his face.
The music's playing, they've kicked off shoes
They're dancing to songs of moulin rouge
Any moment now, their lips will meet.
Though he's still trying to find his feet

But she holds his hand, glove on glove
They are hanging on for love
But…do they know what we see?
Do they know how intrusive society can be?
How their every line will be judged and stared?
And the tiniest detail then compared?

We will measure their every stitch.
Determine which cloth is to go with which,
We'll cut the edges and trim the size,
And when we're done, we'll tag a price.
We'll say he's blue, while she is red
Suggest whom they should love instead,
And pull apart those satin hands
Or…we may give ourselves a chance-
For isn't that what we truly do?
While window shopping we give ourselves anew
In red satin gowns and casual blue suits
Crisp white collars or kicked off boots?

Hoping that when the curtains fall
And the lights go off at Chicago Macy's
We'll find ourselves- glove on glove,
Hanging on for love!

It’s a long goodbye

It’s starting to get dark,
In your brain’s memory arc
There’s a lot that we’ve shared,
But, little that you can recall
You know it’s hidden in there somewhere,
I know it’s hard to find it all

Our lives good,
When we don’t brood over
Little things, forgotten skills, confusing words
Once you walked into the streets alone,
Loving your freedom,
And got me worried all night,
Good folks found you and returned you

As we helplessly meander through this hazy maze,
Every time you are propelled into the ‘I can’t remember’ life’s phase
I watched you leaving,
In your mind always with me,
In my mind you slipping away
I long to have the old you by my side
While, I’m still trying to put together all the puzzle pieces

Hoping life makes sense again
I hope you hold onto the memories as long as you can

We had our plans,
But life had other plans
Now all those dreams are gone
We sit together,
Words from me,
Smiles from you
Your face lights up
Your compassionate touch,
But no words
Cruel dementia
Stealing your memories
But leaving mine!

Lost in life's ocean

I feel like a bird with a broken wing,
With no one to ming (mingle)
I've been blemished by all the wrong around
Hence, I no longer desire any kin to surround
I want to fly away and feel new things,
Perhaps be around new beings
But I'm raged, I can't as yet,
That's probably all I beget

It's a struggle in a swirling river
My body quivers,
Being dragged and juggled
Hope sweeps each passing day along,
Like a glimmer of dazzling sun thrashed against the shore rocks

Some days are hideous,
I just can't focus,
Making my life goals arduous
I pretend to identify the locus,
But have reasons to every season

Please empathise, don't sympathise
Sometimes all I need is your presence

For even your essence
Would dry my tears,
And vanish my fears

Stay by my side,
As I learn to glide
One day at a time,
Together we shall fly
And sore high!!

The not so qualified Maushi

Quick disclaimer - This poem is a satire. All events, characters and entities narrated in the poem are NOT FICTIONAL. Any resemblance or similarity to an actual event, entity or person whether living or dead is PURELY INTENTIONAL.

April to October
Felt like a breeze
Certainly some moments to seize
But a hell lot of people to please

Life's been so tragic:
From being the batch topper,
To now being designated the role of a grass hopper
Those forever long EDs,
Which made me hemiplegic
That failed venepuncture,
I know was a blunder
Those pair of lemon-tinted eyes,
From whom I couldn't hide any further lies
Oh Lord, has all this made me any wise?
From obeying infinite urgent orders,

For which I crossed all borders
Certainly helped me shed those extra pounders
To printing party invitations,
Oh boy, I seriously need a vacation!
From juggling to being juggled,
And devising enumerable escape plans
With my co-intern clan
I've perhaps done it all
Now all I desire is to crawl
Back into my cocoon,
And spin my life's yarn!! (Study)

Let's face it! 🗣️

Don't b a dork,
Coz u r not DNA's replication fork
Y fit in,
When u r born to stand out

With a mighty-powerful arsenal of words,
All u lack is a powerful sword
The dynamic "NO"
You've got to learn (How to say no)
It might burn,
Some relationships
But probably sail your life's ship

It's been so many days in a row
When you've had to slow
U didn't grow
Didn't you reap what u sow?●

So don't let anyone have the remote control to your dreams
Coz not everyone has the genes, (callibre)
That u my queen
Owns!!!💪

I won't give up

When things go wrong, as they sometimes will,
When the road u r trudging on goes uphill,
When all your hopes haze,
When you are lost in life's maze,
When you are broken or probably just frozen
And forlorn is the only companion u have
Stand up right, with all your might
And face them all
Don't let your goals fade

Let go of all dismay
For even the brave,
Have fallen from the cliff of hard times
So U've got to put an end to that sorrowful
cascade
After all, Broken crayons still colour
And life isn't all that duller

Yes, life could manoeuvre you,
With its twists and turns
The blows may hurt
But u must learn
To hide ur bruises
And like a spartan, embrace the war
And never give up,

Though your pace might seem slow,
But, you may succeed another blow

Stick to the fight
When you are hardest hit
U never know how close you are,
Ur goal might be so near, even when it seems so far
So don’t give up!!
Coz there ain’t no chance,
No destiny,
No fate
That can circumvent
The firm resolve of a determined soul

Pure bliss 🕊

U my friend,
Is God's send
If there's anything to mend,
I wish to have known u longer

Those long walks,
Only to achieve 10k steps,
Those weight loss reps,
I wish they lasted longer
Those deep talks,
Possibly made u my folk!

Those dinner convos,
Were sweet mellows
And me leaving my trail (on your bed sheet)
Donning your scarf,
Like a little dwarf ●
Not to forget the derobing blackmail

Those innovative cooking skills,
Which gave u all the thrills
Yeah I would glance,
When I would advance
To hug u from behind

My subtle flex,
And my love for checks,
The way we tease each other just for the heck●
But all aside,
For now u reside,
In my heart ❤

More than a buddy

To my dear friend,
You are my sponge bob-Square pants
The one who listens to my everyday rants
And is inevitably on my daily prayer chants
From being my street smart advisor
And trying to make me "people wiser"
To always always being my well wisher
And unknowingly showing me how to live life with no regrets
Ur the one, without whom my college life would certainly have fissures
From always being caring
And bearing my 'I have to study'
U will forever be more than a buddy
I bet
I couldn't have asked for more

Love you ❤

An ode to my bestie

I miss that human,
My ukulele fine tuning companion
The one who loves to annoy me
And the one,
I could blindly trust when drunk

She knows my weaknesses,
She knows my flaws,
She knows my vulnerability,
She is my weakness, but the one who endlessly strives to keep me going!

We are now continents apart
I can vouch she misses me just as much,
But she's got a strong heart
Who patiently listens to my rants,
And probably has me on her prayer chants

That typical Aries female,
Who eats up all her emotions for weak hearted me
And is so strong willed,
She won't ever let herself lose
Unless she is under influence

I really miss her,
And I appreciate her choosing to be the stronger one!
She’s my dear friend, my soul sister ♥

To me

Don't be a child and weep,
Coz life will seep
Without giving u a beep
So don't be low,
By every blow
One day
U will glow

Don't whine,
U know u have the divine
U know u've worked hard
One day
U will own the trump card

Be addicted to ur passion,
Not distraction
Be strong,
Coz no matter how wrong,
U know wr u belong

Trophies and medals,
Are for those whose feet are always on the pedal
Materialistic people and their needs
Yes, those with never ending greed

My success in life isn't determined by how high
I sore,
But by how grounded I am despite all the
success

All I desire
Is not to sore higher
But for true souls
Who make life worth living for

2023- Travelling and Studying

Everyone looks familiar at the airport these days,
Like a half read book or a forgotten face.
A fleeting look of recognition and then it's gone.
Words almost said, 'It's been so long'
And there are those whose paths would never cross again with mine.
But in the randomness of an airport queue,
Miracles do happen.
So my eyes constantly search for you in a sea of people everytime I fly!

The art of Dissection- 

The first time I held a scalpel in my hand,
And felt the edge slicing through defensive
strands

Of muscle- I watched, as later after layer
Of superficial skins peeled and laid bare

Their secrets- I left the thrill and the string
A careful dissection in formalin can bring.

I was taught to hold the blade like a pen,
Not too tight, not too loose, tilt it right and then

To cut- and if there is blood, pay no heed.
Uncovering the truth is painful. Let it bleed.

I was taught dissection's not just science but art
Whether you are dissecting the brain or the
heart;
Each fibre, each nerve, should be picked up and
pried
Wide open and placed on a microscope slide.

So when I put down my scalpel for a pen in its
stead,

I know I'm still exhuming the dead!

Until we meet again…

A safe place
A warm and fuzzy embrace
A tight squeeze
An oxytocin release
A sense of belonging
Feeling the sun dawning
Arms around each other
My mood lifts
Feelings shift
The bond of much more than just friendship
Clasped tightly
Clinging firmly
Close together
Our souls tethered
My soul sister
Hearts beating as one
For a moment, the world stops
It's nurturing, calm
The feeling lingers one

A hug from you ●

Likes repel, unlikes attract!

●

You and I are like iron filaments,
Lying inert on a table together,
Until a strong electric current
Passed through between us.
Now we find ourselves
In opposite ends of an imaginary magnet,
Stuck to opinions we never thought we'd die for.
That's how a country gets polarised!

The road not taken

As college life comes to an end,
The paths we take may vary,
Some feet rush up the hill;
While others circle; weary.
Yet others just stand still.

And none claims truth or sin,
For all our paths lead in.

Here and now!

The purpose lies in knowing,
But the pleasure lies in not;

The thrill of the chase is in the catching,
Not the caught;

Life finds its meaning, not in the what,
But in the how;

I suggest we live in the here and now!

Goodbye my ♥

It’s time to say adieu
I now feel the separation blues
Don’t you?
Not often do
People walk into our lives
And leave their footprints on our hearts

My heart feels heavy
Life would seem empty
Knowing I soon would be bereft those
Who my eyes would search for in a sea of
people

Goodbye my friend
It’s hard to say
I never thought this would ever end
I hope we meet again
And our paths cross yet again
Until then
I promise to
Hold on and dearly hang on to our friendship
memories!

Thank you for the countless memories ♥

In the pursuit of my dreams

I'm sad to say
I'm on my way
Won't be back for many a day
My heart is down
My head is turning around
I had leave my country to pursue my dream
For I believe,
God has worked his plans for me

I must declare,
My heart is there
But I must go on…
And strive until dawn
For I believe,
God has worked his plans for me

Days are so melancholy,
My mind is numb
But I'm working diligently,
And I hope to never succumb
For I believe,
God has worked his plans for me

All the sacrifices,
The separation pain,

Having to bottle up emotions
The attachments are tough to let go,
For now,
All I know
God is there with me🙏
And we shall Rise and Shine yet again!

www.ingramcontent.com/pod-product-compliance
Lightning Source LLC
LaVergne TN
LVHW020534160826
845677LV00015B/4062

9789358369588